Hot Stuff
to Help Kids
Chill Out:
The
Anger Management
Book

Jerry Wilde, Ph.D.

LGR Publishing
3219 N. W. C St.
Richmond, IN 47374

LGR Publishing
3219 N. W. C St.
Richmond, IN 47374

Hot Stuff to Help Kids Chill Out

For information: LGR Publishing
(800) 369 - 5611

Printing History
First Printing 1997

ISBN : 0 - 9657610 - 0 - 2

PRINTED IN THE UNITED STATES OF AMERICA
10 9 8 7 6 5

Acknowledgments

There are lots of people to thank for helping me with this book. Let's start with Nick Fillmer, one of the world's most bizarre and talented illustrators. Well done, dude!

Thanks also go out to Deanne Gruenberg from the Self-Esteem Shop for inspiring me to keep working on this project and for virtually single-handedly starting my career as a presenter. Everyone should be lucky enough to associate with people who are unbelievably kind and supportive. Deanne has been, and still is, one of those people for me. There's no way I can ever thank her enough.

Dr. James Larson read early drafts of this book and provided much needed feedback. His insights were much appreciated.

Lastly, I want to thank the kids who have shared themselves with me for the past ten years during the many, many hours I've spent working with students. This book is a tribute to all of you because during those sessions, I was the student and you were the teacher.

A Short Note
to the Adults!

Welcome! On behalf of the kids, let me thank you for taking an interest in children and adolescents. As you know, they need it now more than ever. More are dropping out of school, incarcerated, pregnant, and living in poverty now than in any previous era.....sobering thoughts. Oh, that reminds me, there are more kids with drug and alcohol problems today, too. But there is cause to be optimistic because most kids are reachable. Also know that in a lot of cases, concerned counselors and parents like you are the best, and perhaps only, chance these kids have got.

I've tried to make this book very understandable for kids so they can work independently as much as possible. However, there will undoubtedly be times when some assistance will be needed. There is only so much a manual alone can accomplish. The human touch fills in the gaps.

These lessons do not contain numbers (i.e.,

Week 1) because I've found in the past people can feel like slaves to the schedule. We can miss "teachable moments" because there doesn't seem to be time to explore a comment or question. Adults sometimes think, "I've got to get to the end of this chapter and I've only got three minutes!" Please don't make that mistake. Let the kids guide your pace with this material. If a child isn't understanding a certain concept or acquiring a skill, take the time necessary to clear up the confusion.

The pace will also be affected by the effort the kids are willing to put forth. The harder they work, the more progress they will make. Feel free to push when a push is needed but keep in mind the uniqueness of each child or adolescent when it comes to mastering this material.

When I read a book by a so called "expert" I can't help thinking, "I wonder how long it's been since this person has actually counseled a kid or facilitated a group." For what it's worth, I'd like you to know I am in the trenches everyday with kids just like most of you. I ran two groups today at the high school and I've got an anger management group at the middle school tomorrow.   Over the years I've run a couple of hundred groups and counseled thousands of kids so I want you to know these lessons are field tested. I've written two books on anger management prior to this work (Anger Management in Schools: Alternatives to Student Violence - Technomic Publishing and Treating Anger, Anxiety and Depression in Children and Adolescents: A Cognitive-Behavioral Perspective - Taylor & Francis). This is my first book aimed directly at the kids. I hope you find it a useful addition to your professional library.

If you have any questions or comments, I'd enjoy hearing from you. Feel free to call me at (800) 369 - 5611.

Best of luck and keep up the important work that you do!

April 1997

Introduction

You've made a very wise decision. For some reason, you've decided to read this book which could mean several things:

1) You have absolutely nothing to do and are so bored you can't stand it. Reading this book seemed more appealing than taking out the garbage or having your teeth drilled.

2) At this very moment some adult is forcing you to read this book. The choice is either read this book or do homework. After giving it some thought, you chose the book.

3) You were hit in the head during gym class in a game of "bombardment" (also known as dodge ball) and just came to your senses.

4) You want to learn how to control your temper and manage your anger.

I hope the answer was # 4 but even if it was numbers 1, 2, or 3, what the heck....just keep on reading.

These are angry times we're living through.

Everybody seems to be mad at somebody and some people are mad at everybody! Being angry makes it a whole lot harder to enjoy yourself and have a great time in life. One thing I know for sure is that really angry people are not very happy with their lives. Maybe that's one of the reasons you decided to learn more about your anger.

If your keep reading this book I'll make you three promises:

1) You'll have some fun.
2) You'll learn some stuff.
3) You'll still hate to get up early on Saturday morning.

That third one doesn't have anything to do with this book but I just wanted to let you know it'll still be a hassle to get out of bed early on Saturday morning. Here are two more fearless predictions just because I'm in a good mood.

4) Your parents will still bug you about stuff.
5) Your teachers will work you too hard.

None of these come as a shock to you I'll bet.

Before we get going I thought you might like to know a little about me and why I wrote this book.

Name:	Jerry Wilde
Job:	Psychologist
Lives In:	The land of cheese (a.k.a. Wisconsin)
Hair:	Got plenty
Wife:	One (named Polly)
Daughter:	One (Anna)
Cats:	Three (Spazmo, Herb, and Mosh)
Favorite Bands:	AC/DC, Led Zeppelin, Live, Van Morrison
Favorite Movie:	Anything by Monty Python, any movie about baseball
Hobbies:	Listening to music, running, playing guitar, reading books, refusing to be too serious
Cool Things:	Music, sleep, my family, Green Bay Packers, Iowa

Hawkeyes, sunny days,
Diet Mt. Dew

Uncool Things: Ignorance, wasting time,
judgmental people

I decided to write this book because I believe I can help you learn the skills necessary to control your anger, rather than having your anger control you. I've written two other books on anger but they were not for students. This one is just for you, not your teachers, parents or counselors.

Over the years I've worked with hundreds of kids and had a lot of luck with the techniques I'm going to teach you. You can learn to have a less stressful life but it won't be easy. You can have a life that isn't filled with anger related problems but that choice is up to you. If you work hard at the things in this book, your temper will decrease. If you don't work hard, you'll still have the same difficulties you've been having with anger. You are free to choose. You are also free to experience all the unhappiness your heart can bear. I can't and won't stop you. But I'm pretty sure I can help if you do what I recommend.

Managing your anger is like learning any new skill. It takes a lot of hard work and practice. There are absolutely no short cuts but the rewards are worth the effort. Let's move ahead now as you don't have any time to waste. Your anger has probably been slowing, but steadily, hurting your body for quite a few years already. It's time to get to work.

Before we get too far into this, let's take a closer look at the kinds of attitudes you have. Complete the anger survey below as honestly as you can. There are no right or wrong answers, just circle the number which best reflects how strongly you agree or disagree with each statement.

The Anger Survey

Strongly   Strongly
Disagree   Agree

1. I get angry when things don't go as planned.

    1   2   3   4   5   6

2. Other people make me angry.

    1   2   3   4   5   6

3. Life should be fair.

    1   2   3   4   5   6

4. When I don't do well, I get very angry with myself.

    1   2   3   4   5   6

Strongly
Disagree
                           Strongly
                             Agree

5. Things have to be my way or I get angry.

    1   2   3   4   5   6

6. The world has to be a better place to live.

    1   2   3   4   5   6

7. My family can <u>make</u> me get angry.

    1   2   3   4   5   6

8. There are a lot of things that ought
   to be better than they are right now.

    1   2   3   4   5   6

9. I can't control my temper.

    1   2   3   4   5   6

10. I get mad when people don't act like
    I think they should.

    1   2   3   4   5   6

TOTAL_____

The Top 5 Ways Anger is Messing Up Your Life

Chances are you already realize anger is causing problems in your life......why would you be reading this book otherwise? There are many ways anger can mess up your life and we're going to look at the big ones.

Embarrassment

Have you ever done anything really stupid because you were angry? It's okay, be honest. Hey, we all have.

Have you ever called someone a name you wish you could take back?

Have you ever made a complete and total fool of yourself when you've gotten angry?

Have you ever embarrassed your friends or family when you've been ticked off?

When you get really angry, your brain sort of

11

stops working for awhile until you chill out. That's why we do such stupid stuff when we get angry. Take a few minutes and write down some things you've done while angry that you've regretted later.

1._____

_____

2._____

_____

3._____

_____

Some guy named Henry Ward Beecher once said, "Never forget what a man says to you when he's angry." What people say when they are really ticked off is probably what they really, truly think. You can never get in trouble for what you think but once you say something, people can hold it against you for a very long time. Try not to let your mouth start operating before your brain is in gear.

Wasted Time and Energy

Think about this for a minute, What has your anger ever gotten for you?

Has your anger made you any friends? Yes   No

Has anyone ever paid you to get angry? Yes No

Has anger helped you meet cute girl/guy?

Yes   No

Has anyone ever told you, "I think you're really cool because you get mad all the time"? Yes No

Has anyone ever given you free pizza because you get angry easily? Yes No

What has your anger ever gotten you other than into trouble?

That's why I believe anger is usually a waste of time and energy. It never (or rarely) accomplishes anything positive. It does take a lot of work to stay mad. It wastes the energy you need to live, strive and survive. Think about it.

Friendship Problems

Anger also has a way of wrecking your friendships. If you're like most people with anger problems, you have a tendency to fly off the handle. You tend to be sort of unpredictable. It's hard to tell when you're going to go berserk.

Let me tell you a secret. PEOPLE DON'T LIKE THAT!!!! It's no fun being around unpredictable people who fly off the handle and get out of control when they get angry. People with anger problems can become very lonely because after a while they've "gone off" on everyone who was their friend. I don't know about you but I don't like being yelled at........and I don't have "friends" who scream at me. Most people quickly get rid of people who treat them badly and unless you've got a million dollars and can buy your friends, I suggest that you try not to ruin the friendships you have.

Bad Stuff Happens When You Get Angry

Hey, let's be honest here......bad stuff happens when you get ticked off because you act without thinking. Your brain doesn't work right when you get angry. It's true. If you don't believe me, take a look at this drawing of your brain.

This is your brain.

Now take another look at your brain.

This is your brain when you're ANGRY!!!

Anger is Killing You

I know the idea of reading about an experiment is about as thrilling as watching your fingernails grow so I promise I'm only going to tell you about two of these scientific thing-a-ma-jigs. But please, pay close attention because what these scientists found is really important......it could lengthen your life.

The first experiment was on 1800 Western Electric workers who were given a test to measure feelings of anger. The workers were first asked to take this anger test in the late 1950's, way back when Elvis Presley was still skinny. The workers were then watched to determine if higher scores in anger would predict health problems. **The workers who were more angry were one-and-a-half times more likely to develop heart disease and had a higher rate of cancer.** Neither heart disease or cancer is cool.......trust me.

The second experiment followed 255 medical students at the University of North Carolina and

17

began, once again, in the late 1950's. The scientists doing this study found that people who scored higher in anger were **four to five times more likely to develop heart disease and nearly seven times more likely to be dead.** Dying pretty much ruins your weekend.

So even if you're not getting in trouble at school or home and even if you're not having lots of trouble because of your anger.....your body is still suffering.

However, some people still tell you that it's good to "get your anger out" by hitting a pillow or something. They still want to "blow off steam" because they believe that it's healthy to "express your anger." This is WRONG. Ready for the truth? Your body knows **no difference** between anger held in and anger let out. The changes in heart rate and blood pressure are identical. The feelings of anger still cause damage.

The television program "20/20" recently had a segment were they asked couples to discuss a topic they previously fought about. While these couples talked, their blood pressure and heart rates were

18

monitored. Even though they appeared chilly-chill on the outside, their bodies were dealing with their anger. They all had increases in blood pressure and heart rates during the disagreement even though they appeared cool, calm and collected. Their bodies were being hurt by their anger, even when they didn't appear to be angry.

If you think about it for a minute, you can probably find some other ways anger is messing up your life. Write them down below.

1._____

2._____

3._____

So What Causes You To Get Angry Anyway?

This is the million dollar question. What causes you to get ticked off?

Is it your parents?

Is it your brothers and sisters?

Is it your teachers?

Is it your boyfriend/girlfriend?

Is it your dog or cat?

Is it your boss?

Is it a raining day?

Is it the full moon?

Is it a bad hair day?

Is it the price of CDs and video games?

The answer to all these questions is NO. No matter what you think, none of the things mentioned above can MAKE you angry. You, and only you, control how you feel. So the answer to the million dollar question is three little letters. What makes you angry?

Y - O - U

I can hear some of you saying, "Dr. Wilde has definitely gone off the deep end. He doesn't have both oars in the water. The lights are on but nobody's home. He's crazy if he thinks I make myself angry."

Okay......Let me see if I can prove it to you. Let me tell you a story. Let's pretend you were walking down the hall and somebody knocked all your books out of your hands. How would you feel? You'd start singing "Joy to the World", right? No, seriously, you'd probably be angry, right?

But when you turn around to see who hit your books you realize it was a blind student who accidentally bumped into you. Now how would you feel? Still angry? Probably not.

Here's the important part. You still got your books knocked out of your hands so **things happening** (such as dropping your books) can't make you angry. So it must be something else.

That "something else" is your THOUGHTS. Your thoughts, beliefs and ideas are what make you angry.......Not your parents or teachers or family. Let's take a closer look at the example of getting your books knocked out of your hands.

What would you probably be thinking just as your books went flying?

_____

_____

Could it be something like, "You stupid moron. Watch where you're going"? Those thoughts would definitely make anybody angry.

But what would you think to yourself when you saw it was a blind student?

_____

_____

Maybe something like, "He didn't mean to do it. It was an accident." Those thoughts would calm you down.

Notice how the event (getting your books

scattered) stayed the same but the feelings changed as your thoughts changed. That's because YOUR THOUGHTS INFLUENCE (and largely control) YOUR FEELINGS.

This is good news. If other people and things made us angry, what would be the point of trying to learn to handle our anger? There wouldn't be a point because YOU would have no control....other people would be controlling you like a puppet.

Plus, if things happening made you angry, then everybody would be angry at the same things. And we're not, are we? Things that tick off your parents probably make you laugh so it can't be "things" or other people that make you angry.

Now that we've answered the million dollar question, we have our work cut out for us. Now we need to learn how to start hearing our thoughts before we get angry. Not easy, but not impossible.

Some of you still might be wondering about these connections between thoughts and feelings. That's cool. I don't think it's wise to believe anything just because somebody told you it was so. As we'll learn later, it's usually a good idea to look for proof. So let me see if I can convince you that thoughts and feelings are connected by giving you some PROOF.

Below is a list of thoughts. Your job is to tell which feeling would probably go with each thought. My guess is you'll be able to do this pretty easily. Why? Because thoughts DO influence feelings. If they didn't, your answers would be totally different from your friends but I'll bet they'll be mostly the same. Give this a try and see how it goes.

Thoughts and Feelings

What type of feeling would probably happen if you thought:

"Oh, no....I didn't know there was a math test today."
Feeling_____

"What do you mean I'm grounded?"
Feeling_____

"I'm a worthless person."
Feeling_____

"Life stinks."
Feeling_____

"It's not fair that I got a detention from Mr. Smith."
Feeling_____

"I found a ten dollar bill as I was walking down the street."
Feeling_____

"My mom and dad are having an argument."
Feeling_____

See, that wasn't hard to do, was it? Now that you understand the connection between thoughts and feelings, let's move on.

Anger Causing Beliefs

Do you remember the answer to the million dollar question?

What is it that causes you to be angry?

Write it down here.

_____

If you put down "My thoughts cause me to be angry" give yourself a pat on the back and tell everyone, "I'm **way** smart." It's the truth.......lots of adults don't know that they make themselves angry, lots of your teachers probably don't know it either.

But what exact type of thoughts make you angry? Let's find out.

Look at this list of thoughts and put an "X" after the ones that probably cause anger.

1. "People shouldn't be such idiots."_____

2. "I don't like homework but I guess I can

stand it."_____

3. "Even though my parents can be hard to live with, they're not the worst parents in the world."_____

4. "My friends have to listen to what I say. If they don't, they deserve to suffer."_____

5. "My life stinks because people don't do what I tell them to do."_____

6. "This class shouldn't be so hard."_____

7. "I wish my teacher would help me when I'm stuck but I can always ask a friend in study hall for help."_____

If you put an "X" next to # 1, 4, 5, and 6 give yourself another pat on the back and say out loud, "I've got brains I haven't even used yet." Those four statements will probably bring about anger because they all do one thing:

THEY DEMAND SOMETHING

The other statements are still "hoping" something different happens but they're just hoping....not demanding. You've all heard the old saying, "Where there's smoke, there's fire." There's another way to say that with anger in place of fire.

"Where there's a demand, there's anger."

Take a minute and think of a time when you got angry and try to remember what you were demanding. For example, when you got mad for a getting a detention you didn't think you deserved, you were probably demanding two things:

1) That you not get the detention and

2) That you be treated fairly by your teacher.

Does that make sense?

Take an anger example from your life and see if you can figure out what you were demanding.

_____

_____

If you're having a hard time, here are some hints. Look for the "naughty" words that bring about anger. They are:

Should
Shouldn't

Must
Must Not
Have to
Ought to

Can you hear yourself thinking any of those "naughty" words? Any words that are demands will bring about anger.

Some of you may be thinking, "Okay Dr. Wilde, what do YOU think when somebody does something you don't like or you have some really bad luck? Don't you get angry?"

Hey, I get upset just like anybody when someone treats me unfairly or lies about me but what I don't do is DEMAND they treat me better. That's stupid because I DON'T RUN THE UNIVERSE!! And that means I don't control other people.

That's like walking outside on a sunny day and raising my hands up in the air and screaming, "I demand it start raining!!!!" You know what would be even more stupid than that? Getting mad when it doesn't start to rain!

But that's what we're doing when we demand people do what we want or treat us fairly. It's no different than demanding it rain on a sunny day. We have the same control over the weather as we do over other people and things. Sometimes we forget that we don't run the universe.

So what do I do when others treat me badly? I make a wish! (But I don't click my heels together three times like Dorothy in *The Wizard of Oz* though.....at least not in public.) Instead of demanding they treat me better, I WISH and HOPE they will treat me better but I don't get mad about it. Getting mad doesn't change the situation but it sure ruins my day and hurts my body......so I don't get mad very often and I don't stay mad very long.

What's that? You're asking, "What's the big difference between demanding and wishing or preferring?"

Let me tell you another story that may clear up the difference. Let's suppose you had the thought, "I should have $10 in my pocket at all times. If I don't, I'll die." Then you looked in your pocket and you had exactly $10. You'd probably feel relieved, right? But how would you feel if you only had $9? You'd be feeling like Elvis on a diet....FRANTIC, really UPSET. (Sorry to all the Elvis fans, that was the last Elvis joke.)

Now let's say you had this belief, "I would <u>like to</u> have $10 in my pocket but if I don't, it's not the end of the world.....it's not that big a deal. I'd <u>like</u> $10, but I can live with less." You reach in your pocket and pull out $10....cool. Life is good. Later you reach in and pull out $9. Are you going to go crazy? No way. You'll be upset because you'd like to have $10 but you're NOT DEMANDING it so you won't freak out.

The same thing happens with you every time you don't get what you want depending on your belief. If you DEMAND things go your way and they don't, BOOM (instant anger) !!! When you wish and hope things turn out great and they don't.....DARN. That's a shame but, "Oh, well....not the end of the world." See...that's the difference.....you're either in control of your anger or IT is in control of you!

To get good at controlling your anger, you have to get good at telling the difference between rational (true) and irrational (false) beliefs. You'd better be as good as Elvis was at eating banana and peanut butter sandwiches. (Okay, so I lied).

One of the ways to tell if a belief is true (rational) or false (irrational) is to give it the proof test. If a belief is true and rational, there is proof for the belief. It is as simple as that. If there is no proof, the belief is probably false and irrational.

Some of the things we tell ourselves are irrational and not true. Is it possible to know what someone is thinking about you? Is it possible to read someone's mind? The answer is a big, fat, greasy NO!

Anytime you think something like, "I know he's lying about me" or "I know that teacher hates me," you're thinking something that may be untrue. If you hear the teacher say, "I hate you," that's a different story. Then you've got proof!

Can we prove other people SHOULD do what we want? Remember, I'm not saying would we LIKE it if others did as we want. The question is SHOULD they do what we want. Let's look for proof. Is there any proof that teachers, parents or friends SHOULD do what we want? The answer is a big, slimy, hairy NO!

So it is important to think, "Do I have any proof for that thought?" Why? Because nobody wants to tell themselves NONSENSE. And when you believe stuff without proof, you're probably believing nonsense. Hey, we get told lots of nonsense by other people without telling it to ourselves, right?

This practice sheet will help you get better at telling the difference between rational and irrational thoughts.

Rational vs. Irrational Beliefs

DIRECTIONS: Next to each statement write T if the belief is True (rational) and F if the belief is False (irrational).

_____1. I wish I could have gotten a few more hours of sleep last night.

_____2. If I don't do as well as I would have liked in math, it means I'm stupid.

_____3. My parents never let me go anywhere.

_____4. I don't like some subjects as much as others

but I can stand them anyway.

_____5. If I don't get asked to go to prom, I'll die.

_____6. If I wear these old pants, everyone will make fun of me.

_____7. I wish things were easier but they don't have to be.

_____8. I'd like it if my parents would let me stay out later.

_____9. If a teacher gets upset with me, I don't have to think I'm a loser.

_____10. If I didn't get on the honor role I couldn't show my face around here.

_____11. Even if I look like a fool it doesn't mean I am a fool.

_____12. People ought to treat me with the respect I deserve.

Making the Change

Now that you've had some practice telling the difference between rational and irrational thoughts, it is time to take one more step. This practice sheet will give you practice changing irrational demands to rational preferences.......in a nut shell, this is what it is all about.

Once you know how to CONSISTENTLY 1) hear what you think to yourself, 2) tell the difference between rational (true) and irrational (false) beliefs, and 3) change your irrational ideas to rational thoughts, you're well on your way to overcoming your anger problem. Give this practice sheet a try.

Changing the Irrational

DIRECTIONS: Underneath each irrational statement write a new, rational belief.

1. My parents have to treat me the way I want to be treated.

_____

_____

2. I can't take it when things don't go my way.

_____

_____

_____

3. He doesn't have the right to say that to me.

_____

_____

_____

4. You have to help me because I said so.

_____

_____

_____

5. Things never go my way and they should some of the time.

_____

_____

6. My classmates have to take my advice.

_____

_____

_____

7. My grades had better be good or I'll be a complete loser.

_____

_____

_____

8. It would be the worst if I didn't get my way._____

_____

_____

Body Cues

There are certain things that happen in your body right before you get mad. Some of you may not be aware when these "body cues" are happening but it's important that you learn to recognize them. These cues are like a siren warning you just before you go ballistic. By recognizing what happens to your body before you get angry, you'll have a second to chill out before you do something really stupid or say something you'll regret later.

Everybody has some kind of body cue that occurs just before they get angry. Here are a few I've heard over the years. People say they:

- feel warm all over
- make fists with their hands
- have a clenched jaw and hold their teeth very tight
- start shaking all over
- feel their muscles get tight, especially in their arms

Like I said, everybody has a different set of body cues. Think for a moment and then write down what happens in your body just before you get mad.

1._____

2._____

3._____

Now, without looking up, why is it important to know your body cues?

_____

_____

_____

In case you need some help, let's review once more. Knowing how your body feels just before you get angry is important because it will allow you a few seconds to think before you get angry and react. Acting *without* thinking usually leads to bad results.

Some of you may be thinking, "So even if I can recognize what I feel right before I get angry, so what? How is that going to help me? I'll still get mad." Not necessarily.

You'll still get mad if you don't change what you are thinking to yourself. Read the next section for some tips on a way to break your thinking through distraction.

Distraction

Of course the goal of all this is to help you learn how NOT to become angry when things don't go your way. There are things you can do while you're learning these skills to keep yourself out of trouble. One of the best is distraction.

It's simple. You just think of something other than the situation you're getting ticked off about. But you know what happens? When you're getting mad the ONLY thing you seem to be able to think about is the person or situation that's bugging you. It's sort of like when you're starving, pizza is the only thing on your mind. That's why you need to decide what to think about BEFORE you start getting angry.

You need to pick a scene to think about before you get ticked off. This memory should be either the happiest or funniest thing you can remember. For example:

-The time you hit a home run to win a game.
-The time you got the perfect present for
  Christmas.

-Your best birthday party ever.

-The time you said something funny and your
  friends laughed so hard that milk came out of
  their noses.

-The time you had an unexpected day off from
  school because of snow and ice.

I use a scene from a few years ago when one of
my cats named Spazmo tried to steal a hot dog off the
kitchen table. At the time, Spazmo was a little kitten
and the hot dog was almost as big as she was. Spazmo
was dragging it across the floor like it was a log or
something. Every time I imagine Spazmo doing battle
with that hot dog I crack up laughing. There is no
way I could be angry when I think about that scene.

Take a few minutes and think about your
distraction scene then write it down below.

_____

_____

_____

_____

_____

Make certain you've picked a good scene because it is important. Now you need to practice imagining this scene several times daily for the next few days. When you're sitting on the bus or waiting in line to eat lunch just close your eyes and picture your scene as clearly as you can. Bring in all the details that you can possibly remember.

What were the people wearing?
What were the sounds around you?
Were there any smells in the air?
Try to make the scene in your mind just like watching a video.

The idea then is to switch to this scene when you find yourself getting angry. Instead of thinking your parents are acting like jerks, concentrate on your scene. Instead of getting mad because someone borrowed a dollar and forgot to pay you back, concentrate on your scene until the feelings start to subside. Whenever you feel yourself getting angry, switch to your scene.

THERE IS NO WAY YOU CAN THINK OF

YOUR SCENE AND STILL BECOME ANGRY. It is absolutely impossible. Since anger is produced by thinking demanding thoughts, thinking about a funny or happy memory will keep you from getting really upset. It will buy you time to chill. That few seconds of time could be the difference between handling a situation and blowing it.

Right now, think back to a situation where you got very angry. Relive that scene in your mind and feel angry about it just like you did when it happened. Once you're feeling mad, switch to your scene and focus on it like a laser. Keep focusing on your distraction scene.................what happened to your anger? It's gone, isn't it?

My Very Best Trick

Lots of folks have one or two situations where they always seem to blow it........they always lose their cool at the same stuff. If that's you, boy, do I have something cool for you. This is my very best trick so use it with care. If this power were to fall into the wrong hands, there's no telling what evil adults could do with it!

The technique is called rational-emotive imagery and it is very easy to do. Try to imagine a situation where you often get mad.......it could be with a certain friend or family member, it could be with a boss or teacher.

Here's what you do......close your eyes and imagine the scene very clearly. Pretend you are actually there in your mind. See all the things going on in that scene. Hear the sounds that would be around you and everything about the situation. Make it as real as possible.

Next imagine the scene like it is as you get mad. Go ahead and let yourself get good and ticked off just like you would if it were real life. Let yourself feel angry for several seconds.

Now, instead of being really, really mad......calm yourself down. Stay in that scene in your mind but keep working until you get yourself calmed down. When you get to the point where you've gotten your temper under control, take a deep breath and open up your eyes. Below, write down exactly what you thought to yourself to calm yourself down.

_____

_____

_____

_____

If you were able to calm yourself down, chances are you have just written down a rational or true belief. Look at the belief you just wrote down and ask yourself:

1) Can I prove the belief to be true? yes no
2) Is the belief most likely to bring about positive results?   yes no
3) Is the belief likely to get me into or out of trouble?   into trouble   out of trouble

Once you've determined the belief is a true/rational belief, **repeat** the same practice exercise **everyday** and **several times a day** if you can. Practice thinking the true/rational belief you've just recorded when you are trying to calm yourself down. Write it down on a small card and carry it with you for times when you feel yourself beginning to get angry. You can use your pre-selected positive (distraction) scene until you are calmer. Then practice this new, rational thought.

I know, I know...it sounds too simple to work but it does.

I know, I know...it sounds boring. Maybe...but would you rather have more time now or less years to live.

Okay, now it is time to put it all together. Here is your chance to exercise those parts of your brain you haven't even used yet. Try this practice sheet. It will ask you to discover what you were thinking to make yourself angry and change that thought to something that is not a demand. Feel free to return back to earlier chapters to review if you need some help. Good luck!

If you really haven't the faintest idea how to get started, turn to the very end of this book. There is a copy of this worksheet that has already been completed. Please don't copy it because that wouldn't make any sense....your situation won't be like the example in the back but it is okay to look at it to get started.

Anger Incident Practice Sheet

Directions: Complete the practice sheet with as much accuracy as possible. Pretend you are recording this event as if you were a video camera with sound. A video camera couldn't show someone being mean to you. It could show someone calling you names.

1. When did you make yourself angry?
    (What date and time was it?)

2. Where were you when you made yourself angry?

3. Who else was present?

4. As specifically as possible, describe what happened.

5. What did you say to yourself to make yourself
angry? (Hint - Listen to your thoughts and see if you
can hear any SHOULD'S, MUST'S, or OUGHT TO
BE'S)

6. How could you change what you said to yourself to
change your feelings? (Hint - Try changing your
demanding SHOULD'S, etc. to preferences like I
WISH...,IT WOULD BE NICE.....I'D LIKE.)

Successes, Successes, Successes!!!!

It is important that you recognize success when you experience it. Think hard now, have there been times when you've almost gotten really mad and managed to stay in control? By that I don't mean you've been whistling a happy tune....I mean times where you've been irritated but not extremely angry. If so, write down what you thought and did to accomplish this.

Thoughts_____

Actions Taken_____

Have there been times when you've gotten less angry than you would have before reading this book? If so, write down what you thought and did to accomplish this.

Thoughts_____

Actions Taken_____

    Write down any other successes you've made happen because it is important to celebrate victory.

Thoughts_____

Actions Taken_____

    And make no mistake, handling your anger instead of letting it handle you is a victory! Then stand up and say, "I got SKILLS".........because you do.

This is the face of a dude with SKILLS!!!

Now it's time to measure how much you've changed since the start in this book. Once again, complete the anger survey below as honestly as possible. There are no right or wrong answers, just circle the number which best reflects how strongly you agree or disagree with each statement. When you've finished, compare this score with your score earlier in the book. If you're less angry and thinking less demanding thoughts, your score will go DOWN. If you've actually done worse with your anger, your score will go UP.

The Anger Survey

Strongly   Strongly
Disagree   Agree

1. I get angry when things don't go as planned.

   1   2   3   4   5   6

2. Other people make me angry.

   1   2   3   4   5   6

3. Life should be fair.

   1   2   3   4   5   6

4. When I don't do well I get very angry with myself.

    1   2   3   4   5   6

5. Things have to be my way or I get angry.

    1   2   3   4   5   6

6. The world has to be a better place to live.

    1   2   3   4   5   6

7. My family can <u>make</u> me get angry.

    1   2   3   4   5   6

8. There are a lot of things that ought to be better than they are right now.

    1   2   3   4   5   6

9. I can't control my temper.

    1   2   3   4   5   6

10. I get mad when people don't act like

I think they should.

  1   2   3   4   5   6

TOTAL_____

TOTAL from page 10_____

Decreased by _____ Say, "I'm doing better!"
Increased by _____ Say, "I need to work harder!"

Summary

I've done this set of exercises and practice sheets with hundreds of students over the years and I can predict where most of you will be at the finish.

1) Some of you will have made great progress.

You will already be well on your way to controlling your anger instead of letting your anger control you. You've worked hard at the lessons and really PRACTICED. Other people and things don't control how you feel anymore.

2) Some of you will be making progress but still struggling.

You'll understand that you cause yourself to be angry but haven't learned how to keep yourself from getting ticked off. Another way of saying this is, "You can talk the talk, but not walk the walk." You can tell it, but not live it yet.

That's okay. Learning these skills is not easy. You've had a habit of getting angry for a long time and it takes hard work to overcome this tendency. Focus on distracting yourself, explained in an earlier chapter, until you do become better at arguing yourself out of your anger.

3) **Some will feel it is hopeless.**

You might even believe there is now way to ever overcome your anger problems. NOT TRUE. It just takes more work. Think about it this way for a minute.

Whenever you're learning something totally new, there is a time when you can't do it and this new skill seems hopeless. Believe it or not there was a time when you couldn't tie your own shoes!!! You couldn't tell time!!! You couldn't go to the bathroom by yourself!!!

But now hopefully you've all mastered these everyday tasks. So don't give up.

Anger Incident Practice Sheet

Directions: Complete the practice sheet with as much accuracy as is possible. Pretend you are recording this event as if you were a video camera with sound. A video camera couldn't show someone being mean to you. It could show someone calling you names.

1. When did you make yourself angry? (What date and time was it?)
   Last Thursday...around 3:00 p.m.., right after school

2. Where were you when you made yourself angry?
   At my locker

3. Who else was present?
   My friend, Jeff

4. As specifically as possible, describe what happened.
   I asked Jeff to give me a ride to my house so I could get a coat before we went to the baseball game. He said, "No..we don't have time to go out there" and that I didn't need a coat anyway. I got really angry and just sat in the car the whole way to the game without saying anything.

5. What did you say to yourself to make yourself angry? (Hint - Listen to your thoughts and see if you can hear any SHOULD'S, MUST'S, or OUGHT TO BE'S)

He OUGHT to do what I asked him to do. It's not that far out of the way. I do favors for him so he SHOULD do favors for me. He's not being fair and I can't stand it.

6. How could you change what you said to yourself to change your feelings? (Hint - Try changing your demanding SHOULD'S, etc. to preferences like I WISH....,IT WOULD BE NICE.....I'D LIKE.)

I'd like it if he'd take me home but I guess it's really not his fault I forgot a coat. Just because I do favors for him doesn't mean he SHOULD do favors for me...it just means I WANT him to do it and I don't HAVE TO have what I want. It's stupid to get this upset over a coat...I can always ask to borrow one if I'm cold.